Algebra I
and
Algebra II

math
SUCCESS

Rebecca Wingard-Nelson

Enslow Publishers, Inc.

40 Industrial Road	PO Box 38
Box 398	Aldershot
Berkeley Heights, NJ 07922	Hants GU12 6BP
USA	UK

http://www.enslow.com

Copyright © 2004 by Enslow Publishers, Inc.

Library of Congress Cataloging-in-Publication Data

Wingard-Nelson, Rebecca.
Algebra I and algebra II / Rebecca Wingard-Nelson.
     v. cm. — (Math success)
    Includes bibliographical references and index.
    Contents: The coordinate plane — Lines and slope — Linear equations — More linear
equations — Variation — Inequalities — Graphs of inequalities — Absolute value —
Systems and graphing — Solving systems by substitution — Solving systems by elimination
— Systems of inequalities — Systems and problem solving — Relations and functions —
Operations and functions — Exponents — Special exponents — Exponential functions —
Applications of exponential functions — Polynomials — Polynomial operations —
Factoring polynomials — Special polynomials — Quadratic functions — Complete the
square — The quadratic formula — Rationals — Complex rationals.
    ISBN 0-7660-2566-7 (hardcover)
    1. Algebra—Juvenile literature. [1. Algebra.] I. Title. II. Series.
QA155.15.W56   2004
512—dc22
                                              2003027620
Printed in the United States of America

10 9 8 7 6 5 4 3 2 1

Cover Illustration (background): © Corel Corporation

Contents

Introduction

If you were to look up the meaning of the word *mathematics,* you would find that it is the study of numbers, quantities, and shapes and how they relate to each other.

Mathematics is important to all world cultures, including our world of work. The following are just some of the ways in which studying math will help you:

- ▶ You will know how much money you are spending.
- ▶ You will know if the cashier has given you the right amount of change.
- ▶ You will know how to use measurements to build things.
- ▶ Your science classes will be easier and more interesting.
- ▶ You will understand music on a whole new level.
- ▶ You will be able to qualify for and land a rewarding job.

Algebra is an important branch of mathematics. It uses the same operations and numbers that are used in elementary mathematics and helps you apply them to real-life problems and more advanced math problems.

This book has been written so that you can learn Algebra I and Algebra II at your own speed. You can use this book on your own or work together with a friend, tutor, or parent.

Good luck and have fun!

1. The Coordinate Plane

Planes

A plane is a flat surface that continues in all directions. You can think of a plane as a tabletop that extends forever. A coordinate plane or coordinate graph is a plane that is divided into a grid of horizontal and vertical lines.

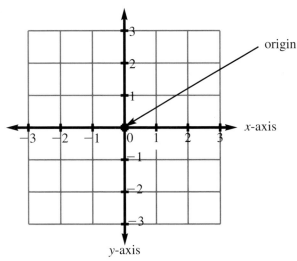

The grid is divided into four sections by two number lines. Each number line is called an axis. The horizontal axis is the *x*-axis and the vertical axis is the *y*-axis. The two axes intersect, or cross, at zero on each. The intersection is called the origin.

Points

A point describes a location on a plane. The symbol for a point is a dot (·). A point may be named using a letter. The position of a point on the coordinate plane is described using an ordered pair of numbers called coordinates. Coordinates of a point are always written in the form (*x*, *y*).

Remember: Coordinates are written as (x, y).

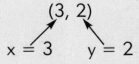

The origin has the coordinates (0, 0). Point C on the graph below has the coordinates (2, −2).

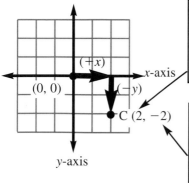

The x-value is 2, so move 2 units right from the origin. When the x-value is negative, move left.

The y-value is −2, so move 2 units down from the origin. When the y-value is positive, move up.

Plot the point G (−3, 4) on a coordinate graph.

Step 1: Draw a coordinate graph.

Step 2: Point G has the coordinates (−3, 4). The x-value is −3. Start at the origin (0, 0) and move 3 spaces left. The y-value is 4. Move 4 spaces up from the x-axis.

Step 3: Draw a dot at the point with the given coordinates. Label the point G.

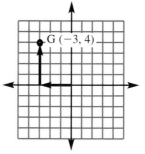

Lines

A line is the shortest distance between two points in a coordinate plane and goes on forever in both directions.

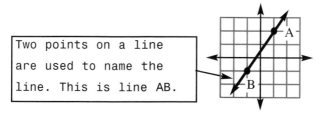

Two points on a line are used to name the line. This is line AB.

A positive x-value moves right. A negative x-value moves left.

A positive y-value moves up. A negative y-value moves down.

2. Lines and Slope

Slope

The slope of a line tells the rate of change. The steepness of the line shows how fast the values are changing. The direction tells if the values are getting larger or smaller. The slope is written as a ratio of how the *y*-value changes to how the *x*-value changes.

Find the slope of the line that passes through the points (2, 1) and (4, 4).

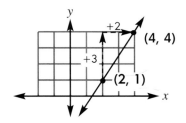

Step 1: Find the change in the *y*-value. The change is found by subtracting the first *y*-value (1) from the second *y*-value (4). $4 - 1 = 3$. The *y*-value goes up 3 units.

Step 2: Find the change in the *x*-value. The change is found by subtracting the first *x*-value (2) from the second *x*-value (4). $4 - 2 = 2$. The *x*-value goes over 2 units.

Step 3: Write the slope as the ratio of the change in *y* to the change in *x*. The slope shows that the line is changing by going up 3 units and right 2 units.

$$\text{Slope} = \frac{\text{change in } y}{\text{change in } x} = \frac{3}{2}$$

From left to right, lines with a positive slope go up, and lines with a negative slope go down.

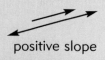

positive slope

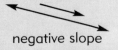

negative slope

Parallel Lines

Lines that are parallel have the same slope because they have the same direction and steepness.

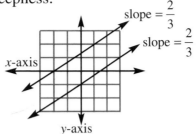

Perpendicular Lines

Lines that are perpendicular have negative reciprocal slopes. The negative reciprocal of a number is found by turning the fraction upside down and changing the sign.

Original	Negative Reciprocal
$\dfrac{3}{2}$	$-\dfrac{2}{3}$

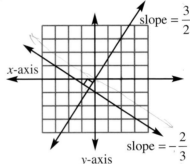

Intercepts

The intercepts of a line are the points where the line crosses the axes. The x-intercept of the line is the point where the line crosses the x-axis, and the y-intercept of the line is the point where the line crosses the y-axis.

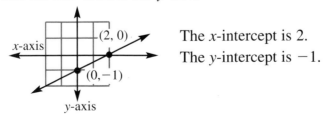

The x-intercept is 2.
The y-intercept is -1.

Lines that are parallel never meet. Lines that are perpendicular meet at a 90-degree, or right, angle.

3. Linear Equations

Graphing a Line

Any line can be graphed if you know just two points on the line.

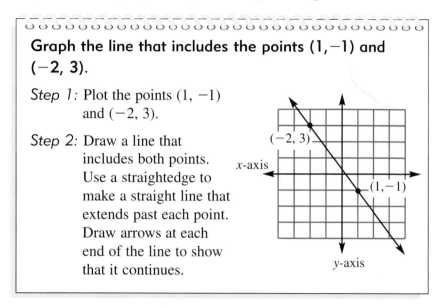

Graph the line that includes the points (1,−1) and (−2, 3).

Step 1: Plot the points (1, −1) and (−2, 3).

Step 2: Draw a line that includes both points. Use a straightedge to make a straight line that extends past each point. Draw arrows at each end of the line to show that it continues.

Linear Equations

A linear equation is an equation that uses two variables (letters) to describe a straight line. Linear equations can be written in different forms.

The standard form of a linear equation is $Ax + By = C$. The letters A, B, and C stand for numbers. In the standard form it is important that A and B are not both zero.

Ax and By are terms in the equation. A and B are coefficients. A coefficient is the number part of a term.

standard form:

$$Ax + By = C$$
$$3x + y = 7$$

A = 3   B = 1   C = 7

Graphing Equations

To graph a line from the standard form of an equation, find the coordinates of two points on the line. The *x*- and *y*-intercepts are easy points to find because one of their coordinates is zero. The *x*-intercept is the point where the *y*-value is zero, (*x*, 0). The *y*-intercept is the point where the *x*-value is zero, (0, *y*).

Graph the line of the equation x − 2y = 4.

Step 1: The equation is in the standard form, A*x* + B*y* = C. A = 1, B = −2, and C = 4. Find the intercepts to graph the line of the equation.

Step 2: To find the *x*-intercept (*x*, 0), put a 0 into the equation for *y*.

$$x - 2y = 4$$
$$x - 2(0) = 4$$
$$x - 0 = 4$$
$$x = 4$$

Now you know that when *y* = 0, *x* = 4. The *x*-intercept is (4, 0).

Step 3: To find the *y*-intercept, put a 0 into the equation for *x*.

$$x - 2y = 4$$
$$(0) - 2y = 4$$
$$-2y = 4$$
$$y = -2$$

Now you know that when *x* = 0, *y* = −2. The *y*-intercept is (0, −2).

Step 4: Now that you have found the coordinates of two points (the intercepts), you can plot the points and draw a line.

Plot the intercepts (4, 0) and (0, −2). Draw a straight line that crosses each intercept. Draw arrows at each end of the line to show that it continues.

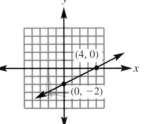

A point is on a line when the coordinates of the point make the sides of the linear equation equal.

The point (2, 1) is on the line with the equation 2x + y = 5 because 2(2) + (1) = 5.

4. More Linear Equations

Slope-Intercept Form

Linear equations can be written in slope-intercept form. From this form of an equation, the slope and the *y*-intercept of the line are easy to find.

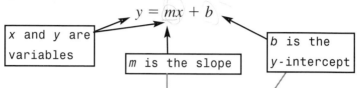

$$y = mx + b$$

| x and y are variables | | b is the y-intercept |

| | m is the slope | |

To graph a line using the slope and *y*-intercept, first locate the *y*-intercept. Then find a second point using the slope.

Graph the equation y = 2x − 3.

Step 1: The equation is in slope-intercept form, $y = mx + b$. Find the slope and the *y*-intercept from the equation. The slope is 2 and the *y*-intercept is −3.

Step 2: Plot the *y*-intercept by drawing a point at (0, −3).

Step 3: Plot a second point using the slope. The slope is 2, or $\frac{2}{1}$. Begin at the *y*-intercept (0, −3) and move 2 units up, then 1 unit right.

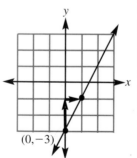

Step 4: Draw a straight line that includes the *y*-intercept and the second point. Draw arrows at each end of the line to show that it continues.

Remember : Slope means $\frac{\text{change in } y}{\text{change in } x}$. A slope of $\frac{2}{1}$ means *y* changes +2 (up 2) and *x* changes +1 (right 1).

Point-Slope Form

The point-slope form of a linear equation is used when you know the slope of the line and the coordinates of any point on the line. The equation is $y - y_1 = m(x - x_1)$. In this equation, m is the slope. The coordinates of the point you know are (x_1, y_1).

A line has a slope of -1 and passes through the point (3, 2). Graph the line. Write the equation of the line in slope-intercept form.

Step 1: Plot the point at (3, 2).

Step 2: Plot a second point on the line by using the slope. The slope is -1, or $\frac{-1}{1}$. Move one unit down, then one unit right. Draw a point.

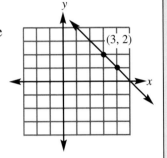

Step 3: Draw a straight line that includes both points. Extend the line past each point. Use arrows at each end of the line to show that it continues.

You have graphed the line.

Step 4: Write the equation in point-slope form. Remember, the points you were given are (3, 2), so $x_1 = 3$ and $y_1 = 2$.

$$y - y_1 = m(x - x_1)$$
$$y - 2 = -1(x - 3)$$

Step 5: Use algebra to put the equation in slope-intercept form.

$$y - 2 = -x + 3$$
$$y = -x + 5$$

The equation of the same line may be written in three different forms: standard form, slope-intercept form, and point-slope form.

5. Direct Variation

Direct variation is a special way that x and y are related. As x changes, y also changes, in direct proportion.

The cost of a number of the pizzas is in direct variation with the number of pizzas you buy. As you buy more, the cost increases in direct proportion.

Number of Pizzas	Total Cost
1	$7
2	$14
3	$21
4	$28

Direct Variation Equations

The constant of variation, k, is the factor that relates x to y. Direct variation equations are written in the form $y = kx$.

Write a direct variation equation for the cost of a number of pizzas where each pizza costs $7.00.

Step 1: Write the direct variation equation. $y = kx$

Step 2: The only value you need to replace is the $y = 7x$
constant of variation, k. The variable y is
the total cost, and x is the number of
pizzas. To find the total cost, you
multiply the number of pizzas by the cost
of each pizza. The cost of each pizza is
the constant of variation, k.

Direct variation equations are linear because they always describe a straight line.

Direct Variation Graphs

In a direct variation equation, whenever the *x*-value is zero, the *y*-value is also zero. All graphs of direct variation equations are straight lines that pass through the origin, the point (0, 0).

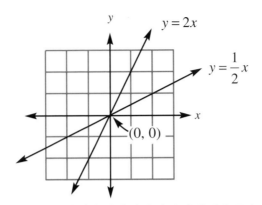

Make a graph of the total cost of a number of pizzas, where each pizza costs $7.00.

Step 1: Write the direct variation equation for the problem.

$$y = 7x$$

Step 2: Direct variation equations all pass through the origin. This is one point on the line. Use the equation to find another point. Use an *x*-value of 1 to find the *y*-value. The point is (1, 7).

$$y = 7x$$
$$y = 7(1)$$
$$y = 7$$

Step 3: Now you know two points on the line. Draw a coordinate graph with a point at the origin and a point at (1, 7).

Step 4: Draw a straight line that includes both points. Label the line with its equation.

When you know two points, you can draw a line.

6. Inequalities

An equation relates two expressions that are equal to each other. An inequality relates two expressions that are not equal to each other.

Symbols

Inequalities use symbols to relate expressions. Notice that in the symbol that looks like an arrow, the smaller end always points at the smaller value.

Symbol	Words
$a < b$ means	a is less than b
$a > b$ means	a is greater than b
$a \le b$ means	a is less than or equal to b
$a \ge b$ means	a is greater than or equal to b
$a \ne b$ means	a is not equal to b

Write an inequality for the following statement:

A cost is no more than $15.

Step 1: Decide which inequality is being used. The phrase "is no more than" is the same as " is less than or equal to." The symbol $\le$ means " is less than or equal to."

Step 2: Change the words to symbols. Use a variable (letter) for the unknown number (cost, c).

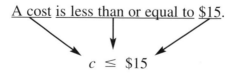

A cost is less than or equal to $15.

$$c \le \$15$$

To help you understand the problem, write the equations and inequalities in words. Then change the words into numbers and symbols.

The answer to an inequality is a called a solution set. For the inequality $x > 2$, any number that is greater than 2 is part of the solution set. The number 2 is not a part of the solution set, because 2 is not greater than 2.

Solving Inequalities

To solve inequalities, follow the same rules as you would for solving equations. What you do to one side of the inequality must be done to the other.

Solve for x. $\qquad$ **2x + 4 < 18**

Step 1: Write the inequality. $\qquad$ $2x + 4 < 18$

Step 2: Subtract 4 from each side. $\qquad$ $2x + \cancel{4} - \cancel{4} < 18 - 4$

$$2x < 14$$

Step 3: Divide both sides by 2. $\qquad$ $\dfrac{\cancel{2}x}{\cancel{2}} < \dfrac{14}{2}$

$$x < 7$$

When multiplying or dividing each side of an inequality by a negative number, you must reverse the inequality sign. For example, the less-than sign becomes the greater-than sign.

Solve for y. $\qquad$ **−2y − 4 ≥ 2**

Step 1: Write the inequality. $\qquad$ $-2y - 4 \geq 2$

Step 2: Add 4 to each side. $\qquad$ $-2y - \cancel{4} + \cancel{4} \geq 2 + 4$

$$-2y \geq 6$$

Step 3: Divide both sides by −2. $\qquad$ $\dfrac{\cancel{-2}y}{\cancel{-2}} \leq \dfrac{6}{-2}$

Reverse the inequality sign. $\qquad$ $y \leq -3$

Remember to change the direction of the inequality sign whenever you multiply or divide both sides by a negative number.

7. Graphs of Inequalities

One-Variable Inequalities

Inequalities that have just one variable can be graphed on a number line. The inequality is graphed as a ray, line segment, or interval.

$$x \leq 2$$

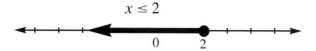

The ray above shows the solution set for $x \leq 2$. The integer 2 is part of the solution set, because 2 is less than or equal to 2. It is shown as a solid dot.

$$x > -3$$

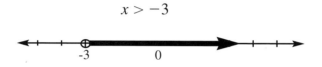

This ray shows the solution set for $x > -3$. The integer -3 is not part of the solution set, because -3 is not greater than -3. An open circle shows that numbers up to, but not including, -3 are part of the solution set.

$$-1 \leq x < 3$$

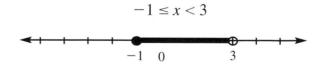

This line segment shows the solution set for $-1 \leq x < 3$. The integer -1 is part of the solution set (solid dot), but the integer 3 is not part of the solution set (open circle).

---

ray—Part of a line with only one endpoint.
line segment—Part of a line with two endpoints.
interval—A line with a segment missing.

ray

line segment
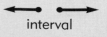
interval

Two-Variable Inequalities

Inequalities with two variables are graphed on a coordinate plane, just like a two-variable equation.

Graph the inequality $2x - y > -4$.

Step 1: A boundary line separates points in the solution set from points that are not in the solution set. To find the boundary line, replace the inequality sign with an equal sign. The boundary line is $2x - y = -4$.

Step 2: Write the equation in slope-intercept form ($y = mx + b$).

$$2x - y = -4$$
$$-y = -2x - 4$$
$$y = 2x + 4$$

The slope is 2 and the y-intercept is (0, 4). Plot the y-intercept and draw the slope (up 2 and over 1). A solid line is used when the line is part of the solution set. Draw a dashed line for the boundary line, because the line is not part of the solution set.

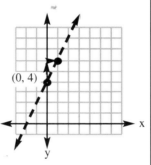

Step 3: Write the inequality with y on the left side by itself. When the sign is less than ($<$) or less than or equal to ($\leq$), shade *below* the boundary line. When the sign is greater than ($>$) or greater than or equal to ($\geq$), shade *above* the boundary line. The sign is $<$, so shade the area below the boundary line.

$$2x - y > -4$$
$$-y > -2x - 4$$
$$y < 2x + 4$$

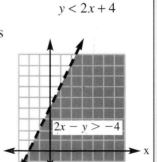

Inequalities are used in real life for things like the height you need to be to ride a certain ride (greater than or equal to 54 inches), or the age that qualifies a person to get a free meal at a restaurant (all children under 3).

8. Absolute Value

Absolute Value of a Number

The absolute value of a number is the distance from that number to zero on the number line. When the number is positive, the absolute value is the same as the number. When the number is negative, the absolute value of the number is the opposite. The symbol $|x|$ means "the absolute value of x."

$|-2| = 2$ because -2 is 2 units from 0.

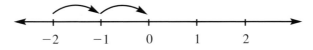

$|2| = 2$ because 2 is 2 units from 0.

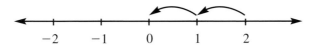

Absolute Value Equations

Solve the equation $|x + 1| = 3$.

Step 1: Break the absolute value into two related equations.

$x + 1 = 3$ or $x + 1 = -3$

Step 2: Solve the two equations using algebra.

$x + 1 = 3$ or $x + 1 = -3$
$x = 2$ or $x = -4$

Step 3: Check your solutions by substituting each into the original equation.

$|x + 1| = 3$ $|x + 1| = 3$
$|2 + 1| = 3$ $|-4 + 1| = 3$
$|3| = 3$ $|-3| = 3$

An absolute value is never negative because an absolute value is a distance.

Remember: Although the quantity inside the absolute value symbols may be negative, the absolute value expression can never equal a negative value. The equation $|x| = -2$ has no meaning.

Absolute Value Graphs

When you are graphing a two-variable absolute value equation like $y = |x|$, remember that y cannot be negative. The graph will never go below the x-axis. Instead, it forms a V shape that sits on the x-axis.

Graph the equation $y = |x|$.

Step 1: The vertex, or point, of the V on an absolute value graph is on the x-axis. Substitute a zero for the y-value to find the x-value of the vertex. The vertex is at $(0, 0)$.

$$y = |x|$$
$$0 = |x|$$
$$0 = x$$

Step 2: Make a table of values for x and y. Use three columns. For every y value there will be two x values: one when the number inside the absolute value is positive, and one when it is negative.

$$y = |x|$$

$y = x$	$y = -x$
$1 = x$	$1 = -x$
	$-1 = x$

y	$x\,(+)$	$x\,(-)$
1	1	-1
2	2	-2

Step 3: Graph the points from the table. Connect the points from the vertex in a V shape. The left side of the V shows when the number inside the absolute value symbol is negative, and the right side shows when it is positive.

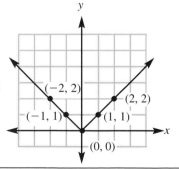

You can use a graphing calculator to find the graph of an absolute value equation. Press the Absolute Value button, then type in the equation. Press the Graph button to see the graph of the equation.

9. Systems and Graphing

Systems of Equations

A set of two or more equations that use two variables is called a system of equations. A bracket ({) is used to show that the equations are a system.

$$\begin{cases} x + y = 4 \\ 2x + y = 5 \end{cases}$$

> Systems are equations that work together.

Graphing Systems

It is easy to find the solution to a system of equations. Just graph each equation on the same coordinate graph. Then look at the two lines.

1. When the lines cross, there is only one solution.
2. When the lines are the same, all of the points on the line are the solution set.
3. When the lines are parallel, there is no solution.

Systems with a solution or solution set are called consistent. Systems that have no solutions are called inconsistent.

See pages 10–13 if you need help graphing linear equations.

Solve the system of equations by graphing. Tell whether the system is consistent or inconsistent.

$$\begin{cases} x + y = 1 \\ 2x - 2y = 6 \end{cases}$$

Step 1: As you learned how to do in previous chapters, graph each equation on the same graph.

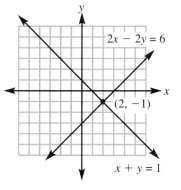

Step 2: Find the point where the lines cross. That point is the solution. Write the solution as an ordered pair.

The solution is $(2, -1)$.

Step 3: It is important that you check your solution in all of the equations, because even if the solution works in one of the equations, it may not work for the others. Check the solution by putting the values from the ordered pair in for x and y, and making sure that all of the equations are true.

$$x + y = 1 \qquad\qquad 2x - 2y = 6$$
$$(2) + (-1) = 1 \qquad\qquad 2(2) - 2(-1) = 6$$
$$1 = 1 \ \checkmark \qquad\qquad 4 - (-2) = 6$$
$$6 = 6 \ \checkmark$$

Step 4: Now that you are sure your solution is correct, you can answer the second part of the problem. Since the lines cross, there is a solution, so the system is consistent.

ordered pair—The coordinates of a point, written in the form (x, y).

10. Solving Systems by Substitution

Sometimes when you graph a system of equations, especially when you graph it by hand, the solution is difficult to read.

When an exact solution is needed, you can find it without using graphing. One way is by substitution. The substitution method replaces a variable with an equivalent expression.

Solve the system of equations using substitution.

$$\begin{cases} 2x + y = -12 \\ \quad y = 2x \end{cases}$$

Step 1: Notice that the second equation has y on one side by itself. You know that the value of y is $2x$. The y in the first equation can be replaced with the expression $2x$. The first equation now becomes: $\quad 2x + 2x = -12$

Step 2: Use algebra to find the value of x.

$$2x + 2x = -12$$
$$4x = -12$$
$$x = -3$$

Step 3: Now that you know the value of x, you can use it to find the value of y. Substitute the value of x into the original equation.

$$2x + y = -12$$
$$2(-3) + y = -12$$
$$-6 + y = -12$$
$$y = -6$$

Step 4: Write the solution as an ordered pair. You found x in step 2, and y in step 3.

The solution is $(-3, -6)$.

Substitution is replacing a variable with an expression that has the same value.

Step 5: Always check your answer by substituting the solution into both original equations.

$$2x + y = -12 \qquad\qquad y = 2x$$
$$2(-3) + (-6) = -12 \qquad -6 = 2(-3)$$
$$-6 + -6 = -12 \qquad\qquad -6 = -6 \checkmark$$
$$-12 = -12 \checkmark$$

Sometimes the original system does not have an equation already in terms of one of the variables.

$$\begin{cases} x - 2y = 20 \\ 3x = 12y + 2 \end{cases}$$

In this system, it is easiest to solve the first equation for *x*, because it is the only variable with a coefficient of 1.

$$x - 2y\ (+\ 2y) = 20$$
$$x - 2y\ (+\ 2y) = 20\ (+\ 2y)$$
$$x = 2y + 20$$

Follow these steps to solve a system of equations using substitution.

1. Solve for one variable in one equation. The variable will be equal to an expression.
2. Substitute the expression into the second equation.
3. Solve the second equation to find the number value of the second variable.
4. Substitute the known value into the original equation.
5. Solve the original equation to find the number value of the first variable.
6. Write the solution as an ordered pair.
7. Check the solution by substituting the ordered pair into each of the original equations.

coefficient—A number that is to be multiplied by a variable.

11. Solving Systems by Elimination

Systems of equations can also be solved using a method called elimination. Elimination uses opposites in two equations to eliminate, or get rid of, one of the variables.

Solve the system of equations using elimination.

$$\begin{cases} 2x - 3y = 8 \\ 5x + 3y = 20 \end{cases}$$

Step 1: Add the equations together. The term $-3y$ in the first equation is the opposite of $+3y$ in the second equation. The opposite terms will eliminate each other. Remember to bring the equal sign down in the same place it appears in the original equations.

$$\begin{array}{r} 2x - 3y = 8 \\ + \ 5x + 3y = 20 \\ \hline 7x \quad\quad = 28 \end{array}$$

Step 2: Once you have eliminated one of the variables, you can solve for the remaining variable.

$$7x = 28$$
$$x = 4$$

Step 3: Substitute the value of the variable you know ($x = 4$) into either of the original equations, then solve for the other variable (y).

$$2x - 3y = 8$$
$$2(4) - 3y = 8$$
$$8 - 3y = 8$$
$$-3y = 0$$
$$y = 0$$

Step 4: Write the solution as an ordered pair. The solution is (4, 0).

term—A number or variable, or a combination of a number and variable. For example:
In the expression $2x - 3y$, the terms are $2x$ and $3y$.

Step 5: Always check your answer by substituting the solution into both original equations.

$$2x - 3y = 8 \qquad\qquad 5x + 3y = 20$$
$$2(4) - 3(0) = 8 \qquad\qquad 5(4) + 3(0) = 20$$
$$8 - 0 = 8 \qquad\qquad 20 + 0 = 20$$
$$8 = 8 \checkmark \qquad\qquad 20 = 20 \checkmark$$

Not all systems of equations have opposite terms. Remember that you can multiply both sides of an equation by the same number without changing the meaning of the equation. By using this property, you can make opposite terms in the equations.

$$\begin{cases} 2x + 3y = 12 \\ x + 4y = 11 \end{cases} \xrightarrow[\text{\scriptsize-2}]{\text{\scriptsize multiply by}} \begin{cases} 2x + 3y = 12 \\ -2(x + 4y) = -2(11) \end{cases} \rightarrow \begin{cases} 2x + 3y = 12 \\ -2x + -8y = -22 \end{cases}$$

The *x* term in the second equation had a coefficient of 1, so the *x* term is the easiest to change and make an opposite. In other systems, you may need to multiply both equations by a number in order to make opposite terms.

$$\begin{cases} 2x - 7y = 3 \xrightarrow{\times(5)} \\ 5x - 4y = -6 \xrightarrow{\times(-2)} \end{cases} \begin{cases} 5(2x - 7y) = 5(3) \\ -2(5x - 4y) = -2(-6) \end{cases} \rightarrow \begin{cases} 10x - 35y = 15 \\ -10x + 8y = 12 \end{cases}$$

It is easier to keep track of what you have done if you write down what you are multiplying each equation by.

Don't give up. Sometimes you may not choose the right numbers the first time. Try it again. As long as you do the same thing to both sides of the equation, the sides are always equal.

Multiplication can be represented using the multiplication sign (×) or a dot (·). For example $a \cdot b$ means *a* times *b*. Often there is no symbol, but multiplication is understood. For example, $3t$ means 3 times *t*.

12. Systems of Inequalities

Inequalities can also be in systems. Systems of inequalities are solved by graphing. Each inequality is graphed, and then they are combined onto one graph.

When you graph each inequality, you must make two decisions:

1. Is the boundary line solid or dashed?

Inequalities that use < or > have dashed boundary lines.
Inequalities that use ≤ or ≥ have solid boundary lines.

2. Which region is supposed to be shaded?

If you are in doubt about where to shade, choose a point and test it. The point (0, 0) is an easy point to check.

Find the solution to the system of inequalities.

$$\begin{cases} x - 2y < 80 \\ x + y \geq 50 \end{cases}$$

Step 1: Graph the first inequality. Use a dotted line, because the line is not included in the solution. For this system, a unit of 10 is easier to graph than a unit of 1. Check the point (0, 0) to see what region needs to be shaded.

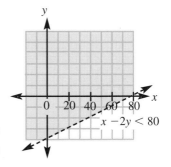

$0 - 2(0) < 80$

$0 < 80$ is true, so shade the area that includes the origin.

Large numbered coordinates, like (40, 50), may be graphed on a coordinate grid with an interval other than 1 between each unit.

Step 2: Graph the second inequality. This inequality needs a solid boundary line. Check the point (0, 0) to see what region needs to be shaded.

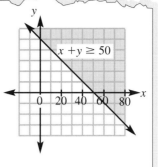

$$0 + 0 \geq 50$$
$$0 \geq 50$$

Not true, so shade the area that does not include the origin.

Step 3: Combine the two graphs. The region that is shaded by both graphs is your solution.

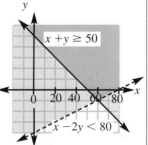

Step 4: Check your solution by choosing a point that is in the double shaded area, and checking it for both inequalities in the system. Remember that on this graph, each unit block is worth 10. The point (50, 50) is in the double shaded area.

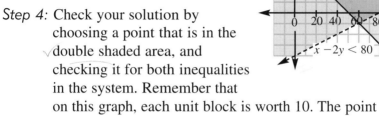

$x - 2y < 80$	$x + y \geq 50$
$(50) - 2(50) < 80$	$(50) + (50) \geq 50$
$50 - 100 < 80$	$100 \geq 50$ ✓
$-50 < 80$ ✓	

Taking one step at a time makes solving systems a breeze!

For more help graphing inequalities, look at pages 18 and 19.

13. Systems and Problem Solving

Some problems deal with a person's age. You can use a system of equations to solve them.

When a problem says "in a number of years," it is a clue to add to the person's present age. When you see "years ago," you should subtract from the person's age.

Helen is 28 years older than her son. In two years she will be 3 times as old as her son. How old is Helen?

Step 1: Set up the equations. Let h = Helen's age now, and s = her son's age now. You are given the fact that Helen is 28 years older than her son, so

$$h = 28 + s$$

In 2 years, she will be 3 times her son's age. For the second equation, add 2 years to each age.

$$h + 2 = 3(s + 2)$$

Step 2: Solve the system. The first equation is in terms of h, so substitution is a good method. Substitute the expression $(28 + s)$ for h in the second equation. Then solve for s.

$$\begin{cases} h = 28 + s \\ h + 2 = 3(s + 2) \end{cases}$$

$$h + 2 = 3(s + 2)$$
$$(28 + s) + 2 = 3(s + 2)$$
$$30 + s = 3s + 6$$
$$24 + s = 3s$$
$$24 = 2s$$
$$12 = s$$

Try solving the age problem using elimination or graphing. Of the three methods, which method did you find easiest?

Step 3: Find Helen's age by putting her son's age into the first equation. Helen is 40 years old.

$$h = 28 + (12)$$
$$h = 40$$

Step 4: Check your answer for each equation. Helen is 40 years old, and her son is 12 years old.

$$h = 28 + s$$
$$40 = 28 + 12$$
$$40 = 40 \checkmark$$

$$h + 2 = 3(s + 2)$$
$$40 + 2 = 3(12 + 2)$$
$$42 = 36 + 6$$
$$42 = 42 \checkmark$$

Some problems deal with coins. You can use a system of equations to solve coin problems. In coin problems, you need to know the value of the coin. For example:

One nickel = 5 cents, so n nickels = $5n$ cents
One dime = 10 cents, so d dimes = $10d$ cents
One quarter = 25 cents, so q quarters = $25q$ cents

Coin problems use one equation to tell the number of coins, and one to tell the value of the coins. For example:

A combination of 5 coins that are quarters and dimes totals 95 cents.

The first equation tells the number of coins. The second tells the value of the coins.

$$\begin{cases} q + d = 5 \\ 25q + 10d = 95 \end{cases}$$

Setting up a table can help you keep track of where variables belong, and it can help you set up the equations.

14. Relations and Functions

Relations

A relation is a connection between two sets of information. For example, in your family, every person has a name. Every person also has a height. The pairing of names and heights is a relation.

> Jim—6 feet
> Wanda—5 feet 3 inches
> Morris—5 feet 1 inch

You can think of a relation as an input-output machine. You can put in one number to find another.

The table shows a relation. You know the cost. Input the amount paid, and the output is the change.

Cost = $1.50	
Amount paid	Change
$3.00	$1.50
$5.00	$3.50

The input number is the domain or x-value, and the output number is the range, or y-value.

> The domain is {$3.00, $5.00, $10.00}.
> The range is {$1.50, $3.50, $8.50}.

The relation can be shown as a set of ordered pairs. A set of ordered pairs is written with brackets around the set, and each ordered pair is written in parentheses.

> The relation is {($3.00, $1.50), ($5.00, $3.50), ($10.00, $8.50)}.

domain—The set of x-values in a relation.
range—The set of y-values in a relation.

Functions

A function is a special kind of relation. It is a relation in which there is only one range value for each domain value. That means for each x-value, there is one and only one y-value.

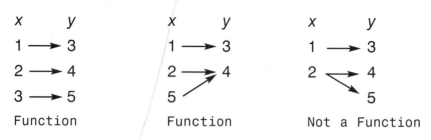

x	y		x	y		x	y
1 → 3			1 → 3			1 → 3	
2 → 4			2 → 4			2 →< 4	
3 → 5			5 →				5
Function			Function			Not a Function	

All three tables show relations. The first two relations are functions because for each x-value, there is only one y-value. The third relation is not a function. For the x-value of 2, there are two y-values, 4 and 5.

Functions may be written in function notation. Function notation is an equation in which y is shown as a function of x.

$$y = 2x$$

is written as: $f(x) = 2x$

and read as: f of x is $2x$.

The expression on the right side of a function is called the function rule. To describe different functions, different letters are used. Different ways to name a function include $f(x)$, $g(x)$, and $h(x)$.

You can replace the x in a function rule with a value you know to find the function of x.

If $f(x) = 2x + 1$ and $x = 2$, then $f(2) = 2(2) + 1 = 5$.
If $f(x) = 2x + 1$ and $x = 3$, then $f(3) = 2(3) + 1 = 7$.

All coordinate graphs show relations, because each x-value has a related y-value.

15. Operations and Functions

Addition and Subtraction

Addition of functions is written as:

$$(f + g)(x)$$

This is the same as:

$$f(x) + g(x)$$

Subtraction of functions is written as:

$$(f - g)(x)$$

This is the same as:

$$f(x) - g(x)$$

Find $(f - g)(x)$ when $f(x) = 3x + 2$ and $g(x) = 3x - 2$.

Step 1: Replace the function with the function rule.

$$(f - g)(x) = f(x) - g(x)$$

Step 2: Solve for $(f - g)(x)$.

Remember to distribute the subtraction sign to each term in $g(x)$.

$$= (3x + 2) - (3x - 2)$$
$$= 3x + 2 - 3x + 2$$
$$= 3x - 3x + 2 + 2$$
$$(f - g)(x) = 4$$

Multiplication

Multiplication of functions is written as:

$$(f \times g)(x)$$

This is the same as:

$$f(x) \times g(x)$$

The commutative property of addition says that you can change the order in an addition problem and the sum will stay the same.

When you are multiplying functions, the most important thing to remember is to use the distributive property. See the following example:

Find $(f \times g)(x)$ when $f(x) = 3x$ and $g(x) = x + 2$.

Step 1: Replace the functions with the function rule.

$$(f \times g)(x) = f(x) \times g(x)$$

Step 2: Remember: The distributive property means you multiply the first term ($3x$) by each term in the second expression (x and 2).

$$= (3x) \times (x + 2)$$
$$= (3x)(x) + (3x)(2)$$
$$(f \times g)(x) = 3x^2 + 6x$$

Division

Division of functions is written as:

$$\left(\frac{f}{g}\right)(x)$$

This is the same as:

$$\frac{f(x)}{g(x)} \text{ or } f(x) \div g(x), \text{ where } x \neq 0$$

Since you cannot divide by a zero, there will be restrictions in division problems. For example:

$$\left(\frac{f}{g}\right)(x), \text{ when } f(x) = x \text{ and } g(x) = x - 2, \text{ is } \frac{f(x)}{g(x)} = \frac{x}{x-2}.$$

The denominator cannot be zero, so $x \neq 2$, because $2 - 2 = 0$. The answer should be written as:

$$\left(\frac{f}{g}\right)(x) = \frac{x}{x-2}, \text{ where } x \neq 2.$$

The commutative property of multiplication says that you can change the order in a multiplication problem and the product will stay the same.

16. Exponents

Exponents are an easy way to show repeated multiplication.

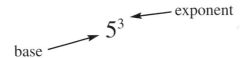

The base gives the number that is being multiplied. The exponent tells you how many times it is being multiplied.

$$5^3 = 5 \times 5 \times 5$$

The value of the exponent is called its power. 5^3 is read as "five to the third power."

Variables are used in powers just as they are in other expressions. A variable may be in the base or in the exponent.

x^5 means $x \times x \times x \times x \times x$ and is read as "x to the fifth power." 4^x means the number 4 multiplied x times and is read as "4 to the x power."

Multiplying and Dividing Exponents

Powers that have the same base but different exponents may be multiplied easily. Just keep the same base, and add the exponents.

$$x^2 \times x^6 = x^{2+6} = x^8$$

Remember: Exponents mean repeated multiplication.

You can see why this works:

$$x^2 \times x^3 = (x \times x) \times (x \times x \times x) = x^5$$

When dividing powers, subtract exponents instead of adding.

$$\frac{x^7}{x^3} = x^{7-3} = x^4$$

You can see why this works:

$$\frac{x^7}{x^3} = \frac{\cancel{x} \times \cancel{x} \times \cancel{x} \times x \times x \times x \times x}{\cancel{x} \times \cancel{x} \times \cancel{x}} = x \times x \times x \times x = x^4$$

Monomials

A monomial contains a constant and a variable, such as $6x$. Some monomials have exponents, such as $6x^2$. Monomials can be products of constants and variables, such as $4x^2y^3$. You can simplify monomials by combining all the like terms.

Simplify $(6x^2)(4x^2y^3)$.

Step 1: Remove the parentheses. Put the constants together, then put the like variables together.

$(6x^2)(4x^2y^3)$
$6x^2\,4x^2y^3$
$(6)(4)(x^2)(x^2)(y^3)$

Step 2: Multiply the constants. Multiply the like variables (x).

$24x^{2+2}y^3$
$24x^4y^3$

Exponent rules make solving problems faster and easier!

37

17. Special Exponents

Negative Exponents

What happens when you divide powers with the same base and the result is negative? Look at the following example.

$$\frac{a^2}{a^7} = a^{(2-7)} = a^{-5} = \frac{1}{a^5}$$

You can see why this works:

$$\frac{a^2}{a^7} = \frac{\cancel{a} \times \cancel{a}}{\cancel{a} \times \cancel{a} \times a \times a \times a \times a \times a} = \frac{1}{a^5}$$

Negative exponents are exponents that are in the denominator of a fraction.

$$a^{-5} \text{ is the same as } \frac{1}{a^5}$$

Zero Exponents

What happens when you multiply powers and the exponents add up to zero? Look at the following example:

$$x^3 \times x^{-3} = x^{3+(-3)} = x^0 = 1$$

You can see why this works:

$$x^3 \times x^{-3} = \frac{\cancel{x} \times \cancel{x} \times \cancel{x}}{\cancel{x} \times \cancel{x} \times \cancel{x}} = \frac{1}{1} = 1 = x^0$$

The only time this does not work is when zero is the base number. Then the answer is zero. Any nonzero number raised to the zero power is equal to one.

base—The part of a power that is the factor.

exponent—The number of times the factor is multiplied.

Powers of −1

When an even number of negative numbers is multiplied, the product is a positive number. $(-1)(-1) = 1$, so $(-1)^2 = 1$.

$$-1 \text{ to any even power} = 1$$
$$(-1)^2 = 1, (-1)^4 = 1, (-1)^6 = 1, (-1)^8 = 1, \ldots,$$

When an odd number of negative numbers is multiplied, their product is a negative number.

$(-1)(-1)(-1) = -1$, so $(-1)^3 = -1$

$$-1 \text{ to any odd power} = -1$$
$$(-1)^3 = -1, (-1)^5 = -1, (-1)^7 = -1, (-1)^9 = -1, \ldots,$$

Power of a Power

Sometimes you may need to raise a power to a power. For example, you may want to raise c^2 to the third power, $(c^2)^3$. When you are raising a power to a power, the base remains the same and the exponents are multiplied.

$$(c^2)^3 = c^{2 \times 3} = c^6$$

You can see why this works:

$$(c^2)^3 = c^2 \times c^2 \times c^2 = c^{2 + 2 + 2} = c^6$$

Power of a Product

When you are raising a product to a power, the power can be distributed to each of the factors.

$$(3ab)^2 = 3ab \times 3ab$$
$$= (3)(3)(a)(a)(b)(b)$$
$$= (3)^2(a)^2(b)^2$$

The exponent gets placed on each factor.

$$(3ab)^2 = 3^2a^2b^2$$

factor—The parts in a multiplication problem that are being multiplied.

product—The result, or answer, of multiplication.

18. Exponential Functions

Sometimes an exponent is a variable, such as 2^x. The variable tells how many times the number 2 is multiplied. Functions that have a variable as an exponent are called exponential functions. $f(x) = 5^x$ is an exponential function.

Look at the graph of the function $f(x) = x + 2$ and the exponential function $f(x) = 2^x$. Remember, the y-value is now called $f(x)$. Graphing a function is the same as graphing an equation. Make a table of values, plot the points, and then connect the points.

x	$f(x) = x + 2$	(x, y)
0	$0 + 2 = 2$	$(0, 2)$
1	$1 + 2 = 3$	$(1, 3)$
2	$2 + 2 = 4$	$(2, 4)$
3	$3 + 2 = 5$	$(3, 5)$

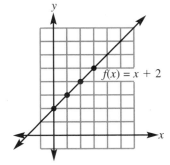

x	$f(x) = 2^x$	(x, y)
-1	$2^{-1} = \frac{1}{2}$	$(-1, \frac{1}{2})$
0	$2^0 = 1$	$(0, 1)$
1	$2^1 = 2$	$(1, 2)$
2	$2^2 = 4$	$(2, 4)$
3	$2^3 = 8$	$(3, 8)$

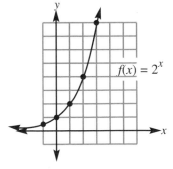

Linear functions form a straight line. Exponential functions are nonlinear, so the graph forms a curve.

Exponential functions are used in biology to model bacterial growth and in geology and archaeology to date items using carbon dating. They are used in statistics to model population growth, and in banking to figure compound interest.

General Growth Formula

The most commonly used exponential formula is the general growth formula.

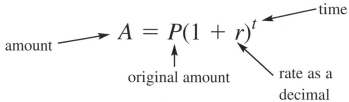

In the exponential growth formula, the rate is a percentage that is written as a decimal. For example, if something is growing at a rate of 100 percent the rate is written as the decimal 1.00. If the growth rate is 250 percent, the rate is 2.50.

A bacterial culture is growing by 100 percent per hour. At noon, there were 5,000 bacteria. How many bacteria will there be at 3 P.M.?

Step 1: Write the general growth formula. Replace the variables with values you are given. The original number of bacteria is 5,000, so P = 5,000. From noon to 3 P.M. is 3 hours, so $t = 3$. The growth rate is 100%, or 1.00 per hour, so $r = 1.00$.

$$A = P(1+r)^t$$
$$A = 5,000(1+1.00)^3$$

Step 2: Use the order of operations to solve for A. Solve inside the parentheses first. Then simplify the exponents. Finally, multiply.

$$A = 5,000(1+1.00)^3$$
$$A = 5,000(2)^3$$
$$A = 5,000(8)$$
$$A = 40,000$$

Step 3: Write the answer in terms of the problem.

There will be 40,000 bacteria in the culture at 3 P.M.

When a number is growing by 100 percent, it is adding its value to itself. For example, when a value of 2 grows by 100 percent, the new value is 4. This is sometimes called doubling.

19. Polynomials

A monomial is an expression with one term. A polynomial has more than one term. Some polynomials have special names.

binomial—two terms: $2x^2 + 3x$ is a binomial.

trinomial—three terms: $2x^2 + 3x - 14$ is a trinomial.

The prefix of each name gives you an idea as to its meaning. *Mono-* means "one," *bi-* means "two," *tri-* means "three," and *poly-* means "many." Not all polynomials have special names.

Degrees

The degree of a term is the value of its exponent. The degree of a polynomial that uses one variable, like x, is the value of the largest exponent.

$4x^5 + 2x^4$ has a degree of 5.

$x + 4$ has a degree of 1. When a variable has no exponent, it has a degree of 1.

$5x^5 + 2x + 6$ has a degree of 5.

Polynomials are normally written in order with the term that has the largest exponent first. This is called descending order.

$5x^3 + x + 4x^5 + 4$ should be written as $4x^5 + 5x^3 + x + 4$.

Terms that have no variable go at the end. In the polynomial above, the term "4" is at the end.

---

expression—A phrase that uses numbers, variables, and operation symbols. An expression does not have an equal sign.

$2x - 4$ is an expression.

Evaluating a Polynomial

Polynomials are evaluated by replacing the variables with given numbers.

Evaluate $n^3 + n - n^2 + 5$ for $n = 0$ and $n = -2$.

Step 1: Put the polynomial into descending order.

$$n^3 - n^2 + n + 5$$

Step 2: Replace the variable with the first given value. Replace n with 0.

$$0^3 - 0^2 + 0 + 5$$

Step 3: Use the order of operations to simplify the result. Zero to any degree is 0.

$$0 - 0 + 0 + 5$$
$$5$$

Step 4: Replace the variable with the second value.

$$n^3 - n^2 + n + 5$$
$$(-2)^3 - (-2)^2 + (-2) + 5$$

Step 5: Use the order of operations to simplify the result.

$$-8 - 4 - 2 + 5$$
$$-9$$

Step 6: Write your answers.

$n^3 - n^2 + n + 5$ when $n = 0$ is 5.

$n^3 - n^2 + n + 5$ when $n = -2$ is -9.

The order of operations is **PEMDAS**
P—Do operations within **P**arentheses
E—Simplify **E**xponents
MD—**M**ultiply or **D**ivide
AS—**A**dd or **S**ubtract

20. Polynomial Operations

Polynomials can be added, subtracted, multiplied, and divided. Polynomials are made up of terms, and some of the terms may be like terms. Like terms are terms that use the same variable to the same degree.

In the polynomial $3x^2 + x - 2x^4 + 6x^2$, the terms $3x^2$ and $6x^2$ are like terms. They both have a degree of 2.

Addition and Subtraction

The like terms in a polynomial can be added and subtracted using the distributive property.

$$3x + 5x = 8x$$
$$6x^2 - 2x^2 = 4x^2$$

Polynomials are considered simplified when they contain no like terms.

Simplify $(3w^2 - 6w) + (4w^2 - 2w)$.

Step 1: Remove the parentheses. $3w^2 - 6w + 4w^2 - 2w$

Step 2: Put like terms next to each other. $\underbrace{3w^2 + 4w^2}\ \underbrace{-6w - 2w}$

Step 3: Combine the terms using the distributive property. $7w^2 - 8w$

Remember: Subtraction is the same as adding the opposite.

$$y - x = y + (-x)$$
$$y - (-x) = y + x$$

Simplify $(3w^2 - 6w) - (4w^2 - 2w)$.

Step 1: Remove the parentheses. Remember to distribute the minus sign to each term in the second polynomial.

$$3w^2 - 6w - (4w^2 - 2w)$$

$$3w^2 - 6w - 4w^2 + 2w$$

Step 2: Put like terms next to each other.

$$\underbrace{3w^2 - 4w^2}\ \underbrace{-6w + 2w}$$

Step 3: Combine the terms using the distributive property.

$$-w^2 - 4w$$

Multiplying a Polynomial and a Monomial

You can multiply polynomials just like you multiply exponents of terms with like bases. When a term has a variable with no degree written, the degree of the term is 1.

$$x \times x^4 = x^{1+4} = x^5$$

When numbers, or coefficients, are used in the term, the numbers are multiplied too.

$$(2x^2)(6x^3) = (2)(6)x^{3+2} = 12x^5$$

To multiply a monomial and a polynomial, you must be sure to distribute the monomial term to each of the terms in the polynomial.

$$(3x^2)(x + 4)$$

$$\underbrace{(3x^2)(x)} + \underbrace{(3x^2)(4)}$$

$$3x^3 + 12x^2$$

Remember: To multiply terms that use the same variable, multiply coefficients and add exponents.

21. Binomial Multiplication

Binomials are polynomials that are made up of two terms. You can multiply two binomials using the distributive property.

Use the distributive property to multiply the binomials $(a + b)$ and $(2a + b)$.

Step 1: Distribute the entire first binomial to each of the terms of the second binomial.

$$(a + b)(2a + b)$$

$$(a + b)(2a) + (a + b)(b)$$

Step 2: Then distribute again.

$$(a + b)(2a) + (a + b)(b)$$

$$(2a)(a) + (2a)(b) + (a)(b) + (b)(b)$$

Step 3: Multiply.

$$2a^2 + 2ab + ab + b^2$$

Step 4: Simplify by combining like terms.

$$2a^2 + 3ab + b^2$$

The FOIL method

A popular way to remember how to multiply binomials is the memory term **FOIL**. This is another way of doing the exact same distribution as we did above.

F— multiply the **F**irst terms
O—multiply the **O**utside terms
I— multiply the **I**nside terms
L— multiply the **L**ast terms

Try writing binomial multiplication using two different colors, one for each binomial. Distribute the binomials, keeping the original colors for each term.

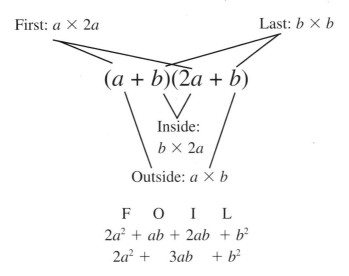

First: $a \times 2a$ Last: $b \times b$

$$(a + b)(2a + b)$$

Inside:
$b \times 2a$

Outside: $a \times b$

F   O   I   L
$2a^2 + ab + 2ab + b^2$
$2a^2 + \quad 3ab \quad + b^2$

Special Binomials

There are three binomial pairs that are called special because their products can be found quickly by remembering how each pair is special.

When the variables are the same but the signs are different, the result is a new binomial.

$$(a+b)(a-b) = a^2 \cancel{-ab} \cancel{+ab} - b^2 = a^2 - b^2$$

When the variables are the same and the signs are the same, the result is a special trinomial.

When the signs are addition:

$$(a+b)(a+b) = a^2 + ab + ab + b^2 = a^2 + 2ab + b^2$$

When the signs are subtraction:

$$(a-b)(a-b) = a^2 - ab - ab + b^2 = a^2 - 2ab + b^2$$

When you use binomial multiplication often, the special products become easier to remember.

22. Factoring Polynomials

When two numbers are multiplied, they are called factors. They form a product. When you factor a polynomial, you find the factors that, when multiplied, make the polynomial.

The GCF

To factor a polynomial, first look for the greatest common factor, or GCF, that is in each of the terms.

$$4x^3 + 16x^2 + 8x$$

Look at the coefficients (numbers) first. The coefficients are 4, 16, and 8. Each is divisible by 4, so the GCF of the coefficients is 4.

Now look at the variables. The variables are x^3, x^2, and x. They are all divisible by x.

Combine the coefficient GCF and the variable GCF. The combined GCF is $4x$. Remember that each of the terms must use the number and variable that is in the GCF.

Once you have found the GCF, divide each of the terms by the GCF and place the GCF outside of parentheses. The results of the division go inside the parentheses.

In the polynomial $4x^3 + 16x^2 + 8x$, the GCF is $4x$, so the factored polynomial is:

$$4x^3 + 16x^2 + 8x = 4x(x^2 + 4x + 2)$$

greatest common factor (GCF)—The largest algebraic term that will evenly divide into a set of algebraic terms.

Binomial Factors

Sometimes polynomials have a common factor that is a binomial. A binomial factor can be removed just like a monomial factor, using the distributive property.

Factor the polynomial $a(b - 4) + 5(b - 4)$.

Step 1: Write the polynomial. You can see that each term has a factor of $(b - 4)$.

$$a(b - 4) + 5(b - 4)$$

Step 2: Factor out the common binomial $(b - 4)$.

$$(b - 4)(a + 5)$$

Factor by Grouping

When some of the terms in a polynomial have common numbers or variables, they can be grouped and treated as a separate expression.

In the polynomial $m^2 + m + 2m + 2$, separate the first two terms from the second two terms.

$$(m^2 + m) + (2m + 2)$$

The first two terms have a common factor of m, and the second two terms have a common factor of 2. Use the distributive property to remove the common factors.

$$m(m + 1) + 2(m + 1)$$

Factor out the common binomial from each term.

$$(m + 2)(m + 1)$$

There are no longer any common factors, so the polynomial is factored.

Some polynomials use more than one factoring method. After factoring out a GCF, look for terms that can be grouped.

Factoring polynomials undoes the multiplication of polynomials that is on pages 45–47.

23. Special Polynomials

There are polynomials that can be easily factored once they are recognized as special. The pattern of the terms can help you recognize each special type.

Perfect-Square Trinomials

The trinomial $x^2 + 2xy + y^2 = (x + y)(x + y) = (x + y)^2$.
Look at the picture of the square.

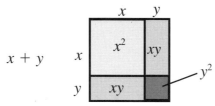

The area of a square is $(side)^2$. To find the area of this square, the side length is $x + y$, so:
$$\text{Area} = (\text{side})^2 = (x + y)^2$$
The area may also be found by finding the area of each of the parts, then adding them together.
$$x^2 + xy + xy + y^2 = x^2 + 2xy + y^2$$
Both methods will find the area of a square with the side length of $x + y$.

If you look closely at the trinomial, you can see that the first term is a perfect square and the final term is a perfect square. The middle term is twice the product of the square root of the first and last term.

The first term is x^2. $\sqrt{x^2} = x$. The last term is y^2. $\sqrt{y^2} = y$.
Twice the product of these square roots is $2(x)(y)$, or $2xy$.

A square root is the number that, when multiplied by itself, produces the number under the square root symbol. The square root of 9, or $\sqrt{9}$, equals 3 because $3 \times 3 = 9$.

When the middle term of a perfect square trinomial is negative, the sign of the squared binomial is subtraction.

$$a^2 - 2ab + b^2 = (a - b)(a - b) = (a - b)^2$$

The Difference of Two Squares

When you multiply $(a + b)(a - b)$, the product is $a^2 - b^2$. The product $(a^2 - b^2)$ is called the difference of two squares.

This is an easy special polynomial to recognize and factor. There will be only two terms, and both terms are perfect squares. The polynomial must be the difference, and not a sum.

$a^2 + b^2$ is not the difference of two squares.
It is a sum.
$a^2 - 6b^2$ is not the difference of two squares.
The term $6b^2$ is not a perfect square.

Factor the polynomial $9x^2 - 4$.

Step 1: Write the polynomial. $\qquad 9x^2 - 4$

Step 2: The polynomial has two terms, and is a difference. Check each term to see if it is a perfect square.
$9x^2 = (3x)^2 \qquad 4 = (2)^2$
Yes $\qquad\qquad$ Yes

Step 3: Since the polynomial is the difference of two squares, one factor is the addition of the two square roots $(3x + 2)$. The other factor is the first square root minus the second square root $(3x - 2)$.

Step 3: Write the solution.

$$9x^2 - 4 = (3x + 2)(3x - 2)$$

Perfect squares are the result of multiplying a whole number by itself. 9 is a perfect square because $3 \times 3 = 9$, and 3 is a whole number.

24. Quadratic Functions

Quadratic functions are a special type of polynomial function whose highest power is 2. The functions $f(x) = x^2$ and $f(x) = 2x^2 - 3x + 1$ are both examples of quadratic functions.

A quadratic function is easy to recognize by its equation. The standard form of a quadratic function is:

$$f(x) = ax^2 + bx + c, \text{ where } a \neq 0$$

Vertex Form

An important form of quadratic equations is vertex form. To understand vertex form, you need to recognize the graph of a quadratic function. All quadratic functions have a U-shaped graph that is called a parabola.

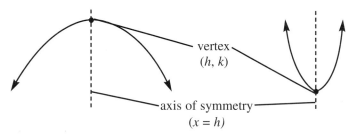

vertex
(h, k)

axis of symmetry
$(x = h)$

A parabola is made up of two halves that are exact reflections. The vertex of a parabola is the lowest or highest point where the parabola begins to change direction. The vertical line that goes through the center of the vertex is called the axis of symmetry.

The vertex form of a quadratic function is written in the form

$$y = a(x - h)^2 + k$$

Look on pages 48−51 for help in factoring polynomials.

In the vertex form of a quadratic equation, the point (h, k) is the vertex. The line $x = h$ is the axis of symmetry. If a is a positive number, the parabola opens upward. If a is a negative number, the parabola opens downward.

Identify the vertex and axis of symmetry for the graph of $y = -(x - 3)^2 + 4$. Tell whether the parabola opens upward or downward.

Step 1: Write the equation in vertex form. This equation is already in vertex form.

$$y = a(x - h)^2 + k$$
$$y = -(x - 3)^2 + 4$$

Step 2: Identify the values for a, h, and k.

$$y = -(x - 3)^2 + 4$$
is the same as
$$y = -1(x - 3)^2 + 4$$

$a = -1 \qquad h = 3 \qquad k = 4$

Step 3: Identify the vertex. The vertex is the point (h, k). The vertex of the parabola is at point $(3, 4)$.

Step 4: Identify the axis of symmetry. The axis of symmetry is the vertical line that runs through the center of the parabola. The equation of the axis of symmetry is $x = h$.

The axis of symmetry for the parabola is $x = 3$.

Step 5: When a is positive, the parabola opens upward. When a is negative, the parabola opens downward.

Since $a = -1$, the parabola opens downward.

axis of symmetry—The line through the center of a figure that divides it into two equal halves that mirror each other. If you fold a figure along the axis of symmetry, both sides are exactly the same in size and shape.

25. Complete the Square

To graph a quadratic function, get it into vertex form. Often a quadratic function will not go nicely into vertex form, and you will need to do something called completing the square first.

Let's look at the quadratic function $f(x) = x^2 + 4x$.
First, find the number you need to add to the function to make $x^2 + 4x$ a perfect-square trinomial. Look at the figures below.

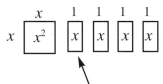

Each of the figures marked x has a side of x, a side length of 1 unit, and an area of x. In order to create a perfect square, move two of the x areas below the x^2. This gives you the beginning of a square with a side length of $x + 2$.

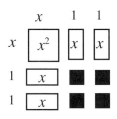

To make a complete square, you need to add one-unit squares. Four one-unit squares will make this square complete. You can make a perfect square trinomial the same way.

$x^2 + 4x$ is not a perfect square, but if you add 4, it becomes the perfect-square trinomial $x^2 + 4x + 4$. You will subtract this 4 in the next step, so the value of the expression will not change.

Remember: Perfect-square trinomials are the result of squaring a binomial, or multiplying the binomial by itself.

Writing in Vertex Form

You can write a quadratic equation in vertex form by completing the square.

Write the equation $f(x) = x^2 - 8x + 5$ in vertex form.

Step 1: Write the quadratic equation. $\qquad f(x) = x^2 - 8x + 5$

Step 2: To complete a square you must start with a binomial in the form $x^2 + bx$. Group the terms in the quadratic that are in that form. $\qquad f(x) = (x^2 - 8x) + 5$

Step 3: Use the coefficient of the x-term to find the number you need to add in order to make a perfect trinomial. In this example, the x-term has a coefficient of -8. Half of -8 is -4. $(-4)^2$ is 16.

Step 4: Complete the square. Add the number you found (16) inside the parentheses that you made when you grouped the terms. When you add a number inside the parentheses, you must subtract the same number (16) outside the parentheses.

$$f(x) = (x^2 - 8x + 16) + 5 - 16$$

Step 5: Simplify the function. $\qquad f(x) = (x^2 - 8x + 16) - 11$
Now you have a perfect square trinomial inside the parentheses.

$$f(x) = (\underbrace{x^2 - 8x + 16}_{(x-4)^2}) - 11 = (x-4)^2 - 11$$

Step 6: Write the function in vertex form. $\qquad y = (x - 4)^2 - 11$
The vertex form of an equation is $y = a(x - h)^2 + k$. Remember that $f(x)$ is the same as y. In this equation, $a = 1$, $h = 4$, and $k = 11$.

For more information on the vertex form of a quadratic function, look at pages 52 and 53.

26. The Quadratic Formula

The quadratic formula is used to find the solution to quadratic equations. The quadratic formula is:

$$x = \frac{-b \pm \sqrt{b^2 - 4ac}}{2a} \text{ for } ax^2 + bx + c = 0, \text{ where } a \neq 0$$

There are two important parts to using the quadratic formula for solving for x. They are:

1. You need to know the formula. Most of the time if you do not have the formula memorized, you will find that it is written out in the problem or near the problem in your textbook.

2. Identify the coefficients a and b and the constant c. Both b and c can be zero or one, so you need to be careful to identify these.

$$2x^2 - 3x + 9 = 0$$

$$a = 2 \quad b = -3 \quad c = 9$$

$$x^2 + x = 0$$

is the same as

$$(1)x^2 + (1)x + 0 = 0$$

$$a = 1 \quad b = 1 \quad c = 0$$

When you know the values for a, b, and c, substitute the numbers for the variables and solve for x.

---

solution—The set of values that makes an equation a true statement.

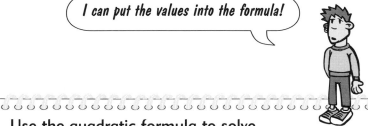

I can put the values into the formula!

Use the quadratic formula to solve $2x^2 + 2 + 4x = 0$.

Step 1: Rewrite the equation in the standard form of $x^2 + bx + c = 0$

$2x^2 + 4x + 2 = 0$

Step 2: Identify the coefficients and the constant.

$a = 2, \quad b = 4, c = 2$

Step 3: Write the quadratic formula.

$$x = \frac{-b \pm \sqrt{b^2 - 4ac}}{2a}$$

Step 4: Substitute the values into the formula.

$$x = \frac{-4 \pm \sqrt{4^2 - 4(2)(2)}}{2(2)}$$

Step 5: Simplify the expression on the right side.

$$x = \frac{-4 \pm \sqrt{16 - 16}}{4}$$

$$x = \frac{-4 \pm 0}{4}$$

$$x = -1$$

Step 6: Check your solution by substituting it into the original equation.

$2x^2 + 4x + 2 = 0$
$2(-1)^2 + 4(-1) + 2 = 0$
$2 - 4 + 2 = 0$
$0 = 0$

Remember to always check your solution by putting the solution into the original equation.

27. Rationals

A rational expression is a fraction of two polynomials. A rational function is the function of a rational expression.

$$\frac{x+4}{2x-3} \text{ is a rational expression.}$$

$$f(x) = \frac{x+4}{2x-3} \text{ is a rational function.}$$

Simplifying Rational Expressions

To simplify a rational expression, divide the numerator and denominator by a common factor. It helps if you factor the polynomials first. That way you can identify the common factors more easily.

Simplify the rational expression $\dfrac{4x^2 + 8x + 4}{x+1}$.

Step 1: Write the rational expression.

$$\frac{4x^2 + 8x + 4}{x+1}$$

Step 2: Factor the numerator and denominator.

$$\frac{4(x^2 + 2x + 1)}{x+1}$$

$$\frac{4(x+1)(x+1)}{x+1}$$

Step 3: Cancel out the common factors in the numerator and denominator.

$$\frac{4(x+1)(x\!\!\!\not{+1})}{x\!\!\!\not{+1}}$$

Write the result.

$$4(x + 1)$$

Step 4: Simplify the remaining expression. This is the solution.

$$4x + 4$$

numerator—The top part of a fraction.
denominator—The bottom part of a fraction.

Rational Operations

Multiplying and dividing rational expressions is done the same way as multiplying and dividing fractions.

To multiply rational expressions, multiply the numerators. Then multiply the denominators.

$$\frac{x+1}{x} \cdot \frac{2x^3}{x+1} = \frac{\cancel{x+1}}{x} \cdot \frac{2x^3}{\cancel{x+1}} = \frac{2x^{\cancel{3}\,2}}{\cancel{x}} = 2x^2$$

To divide rational expressions, multiply the first expression by the inverse of the second expression.

$$\frac{81}{x-2} \div \frac{9}{x} = \frac{81}{x-2} \cdot \frac{x}{9} = \frac{^9\cancel{(81)}(x)}{(x-2)(\cancel{9})} = \frac{9x}{x-2}$$

Adding and subtracting rational expressions with the same denominator is the same as adding or subtracting fractions with the same denominator. The denominator remains the same, and you add or subtract the numerator.

$$\frac{2x}{(x-9)} + \frac{3}{(x-9)} = \frac{2x+3}{(x-9)}$$

$$\frac{x^2}{(x-1)} - \frac{x}{(x-1)} = \frac{x^2-x}{(x-1)} = \frac{x(\cancel{x-1})}{(\cancel{x-1})} = x$$

After you do any operations on rational expressions, always reduce the expression to its lowest terms.

Put binomials in parentheses to avoid confusion. (x + 2)

28. Complex Rationals

A complex rational is a special type of fraction. It has fractions in the numerator, denominator, or both. You can add, subtract, multiply, and divide complex fractions just like regular fractions.

$$\dfrac{\left(\dfrac{2x+4}{x-7}\right)}{\left(\dfrac{x+2}{x+3}\right)}$$

$\left.\vphantom{\dfrac{2x+4}{x-7}}\right\}$ numerator

$\left.\vphantom{\dfrac{x+2}{x+3}}\right\}$ denominator

Simplify the complex rational $\dfrac{\left(\dfrac{2x+4}{x-7}\right)}{\left(\dfrac{x+2}{x+3}\right)}$.

Step 1: Write the fraction as a division problem.

$$\dfrac{2x+4}{x-7} \div \dfrac{x+2}{x+3}$$

Step 2: Division is the same as multiplication by the reciprocal. Flip the second fraction and change the division sign to a multiplication sign.

$$\dfrac{2x+4}{x-7} \bullet \dfrac{x+3}{x+2}$$

Step 3: Multiply the fractions. The terms should be written in factored form.

$$\dfrac{(2x+4)(x+3)}{(x-7)(x+2)}$$

$$\dfrac{2(x+2)(x+3)}{(x-7)(x+2)}$$

factored form—An expression written in terms of its factors.
2x + 4 is 2(x + 2) in factored form.

Step 4: Cancel out any common factors in the numerator and denominator.	$\dfrac{2(\cancel{x+2})(x+3)}{(x-7)(\cancel{x+2})}$
	$\dfrac{2(x+3)}{(x-7)}$
Step 5: Simplify and write the solution.	$\dfrac{2x+6}{x-7}$

The key to solving complex rationals is to take it one step at a time, and try not to get flustered.

Follow these steps to solve a complex rational:

1. Rewrite the complex rational as a division problem.
2. Change the division to multiplication by multiplying by the reciprocal of the second rational.
3. Break each term into its factors so that it is easier to spot common factors in the numerator and denominator.
4. Divide out any common factors.
5. Simplify the remaining expression. In this step, combine any factors that have like terms.

simplify—To remove all parentheses and combine the like terms in an expression.

Further Reading

Books

Jund, Barbara. *Algebra Success in 20 Minutes a Day.* New York: Learning Express, Inc., 2000.

Kaplan, Andrew. *Algebra to Go: A Mathematics Handbook.* Wilmington, Mass.: Great Source Education Group Inc., 2000.

Long, Lynette. *Painless Algebra.* Hauppauge, N.Y.: Barron's Educational Series, Inc., 1998.

Rappaport, Josh. *Algebra Survival Guide: A Conversational Guide for the Thoroughly Befuddled.* Santa Fe, N.M.: Singing Turtle Press, 1999.

Schadler, Reuben. *Algebra Problems: One Step Beyond.* White Plains, N.Y.: Dale Seymour Publications, 1997.

Internet Addresses

Webmath. *Webmath.* © 2003. <http://www.webmath.com>.

Math League Multimedia. *Introduction to Algebra.*
© 1997– 2001.
<http://www.mathleague.com/help/algebra/algebra.htm>.

Stapel, Elizabeth. *Purplemath—Your Algebra Resource.*
© 2000–2004.
<http://www.purplemath.com/modules/translat.htm>.

Index